Paul Samuels

EXPRESSIONS
OF LIFE

Paul Leon Samuels

DEDICATION

To Arlene Bridges Samuels, my wife, best friend and companion since 1976. You have encouraged me to be a better man, father and writer than I ever thought I could be. Truly there is no better description than to say you are indeed a Proverbs 31:10-12 wife!

To Chad and Gloria Grace, our miracle adoption gifts from God.

ALSO

Special thanks to Arlene Bridges Samuels and Bob Dahlgren who worked hours and hours to make this book happen. Also my thanks to a few friends who proof read and caught the places which needed to be corrected.

TABLE OF EXPRESSIONS

ABOUT MY RETRO COVER

In the 1950's and '60s, when I was growing up, brick walls, sides of buildings, and sidewalks served as canvases where people could express themselves. Announcements in large letters about tourist destinations ahead appeared on rooftops. Billboards, then and now, littered roadways to sell us any and everything.

Back in the mid- seventies, I chose this brick wall to express sentiments and friendships for the book I am now finally writing almost forty years later!

With the advent of the world wide web, more opportunities to express ourselves artistically and in social networks dominate the world of communications. Bottom line-then and now-people want to express themselves. The human need to communicate-to be heard and understood-pervades all relationships.

Some in social media simply live to pick a fight and take the opposing side of whatever comes along. Then others take the high road of help offering counsel and opinions to help others move through the various problems we all face.

It's truly comforting to read how others deal with their life situations, possibly because when we face a rough time there is a tendency to feel like we are alone in our suffering and no one else understands. Knowing how others deal with life is helpful and encouraging regardless of our various religious beliefs.

My book is about a myriad of experiences I have either gone through myself or stood close enough to those going through them to capture their thoughts & emotions. It is by no means meant to be a remedy for everything nor a suggestion of the correct ways to handle life's curve balls. It is simply a collection of life's expressions.

Family and friends have encouraged me to put my poems together in book form. They haven't anointed me as a "Great Literary Poet" but rather a "People's Poet" who can identify with life's experiences without the usual backdrop of academia. It is my earnest hope that on each page you will encounter insight, comfort, joy, peace and- perhaps help-to walk with your head held a little higher and your steps a little lighter on your life's journey.

ABOUT THE AUTHOR

Growing up on the streets of the South Bronx served as a harsh palate for my almost desperate search for meaning. In the poetry from James Kavanaugh, Rod McKuen and the songs of Bob Dylan and Harry Chapin, I found solace and an expressive outlet to re-set my thoughts in the direction of beauty and a positive outlook on life. Four years in the U.S. Navy also helped to give me more of a world outlook.

My life is a kaleidoscope of variety from a not-so-good beginning to my present home in Georgia. Like most of us, I've known pain and despair and yet experienced God turning ashes into beauty in ways I never anticipated. I've enjoyed the privilege of serving in missions with Youth With A Mission, Mercy Ships, Messianic Jewish Alliance of America, and World Vision.

I've traveled the world making my small contributions to the lives of those less fortunate, turning my own background into a tool for good. Living on a hospital ship, and living in Romania, and Switzerland, I've found ways to contribute to our world. On our own soil-and in more ordinary locations, add to that Hilton Head Island, Charlotte, NC, Van, Texas, Mt. Pleasant, SC. and Atlanta, Ga. I maintain a license as a Real Estate Broker (since 1980) and as a licensed Instructor since 2003. I do not practice at this time as I am retired.

I'm a husband a dad and granddad. If money was the measuring stick of my life's success, I'd be counted a failure. But if living every day in the fullness of my "relationships" and life adventures then I'm a success.

I spend most of my time serving as what my wife refers to as her "chief of staff" as well as Mr. House Butler. I have the privilege of being her chauffer and assisting her in the background of her very demanding and wonderful position. While "behind every successful man is a good woman" may be a cliché it is also the truth. Years of marriage to Arlene Bridges, the former Miss Florence, SC, have been the best years of my life. I sometimes wonder what direction my life would have taken without Arlene's love and support. She is the epitome of love, loyalty, and dedication. She is my soul mate and my best friend. She is also a classic and consistent example of scripture's admonition to forgive 70x7. I've given her much practice.

I am also author of a children's book entitled Where is Christmas? Both books are on Amazon.com as well as my web page.

Adoption has been a profound gift from God for Arlene and me. In 1988 we adopted Chad when he was 5 days old in Charleston, SC. Then in 1991, we traveled to Romania to adopt a tiny, beautiful Gloria Grace, who was 28 days old. My life is rich in love!

Want to communicate? www.paulsamuels.com

AH SUBSTANCE!

(My viewpoint on writing poetry.)

Poetry is to the reader as beauty is to the beholder. There are those who try to dictate what beauty is for others; there are also those who attempt it with poetry.

Is a grey haired, wrinkle-faced wife of sixty years less beautiful to the groom who still stands by her side? Is a tired old man leaning heavily on his cane any less of a man to the bride he swept off her feet?

Their form may have changed but the substance of their love remains intact. "Form" is good but the ultimate in love- or poetry- is substance.

Some poets format words to their pattern of choice, and others rave about the form in order to "belong" yet never understanding the substance. Some are so intimidated by the challenge of meeting the form that the substance remains lost.

Words have power to paint a picture of substance in the mind of the reader. The essence of poetry is to condense much into little and to empower the " little" to explode with vision and feeling for the reader. Substance!

What matters form if you "feel the coolness of the wind blowing through your hair" as you read what I'm experiencing? What matters form if you "notice the ever changing scents of the air you breathe" when you are reading how I notice.

Poetry is the essence of our thoughts and experiences poured onto the empty page taking the hearts and minds of those who read it on the journey beside us.

Never, never, never, let someone else's judgment of the form, or your desire to write "acceptably" keep you from serving up the substance of what you think and feel and what you have seen.

Write, Write, Write!

And share the substance of your experiences in life.

QUESTIONS
I'VE
ASKED

RAMBLING THOUGHTS

I have no true goal, at least not a goal as the world would call it. I don't want to be rich beyond imagination although at times I do want what money can buy. I don't want great amounts of responsibility although at times I do want the recognition and the fame which goes along with it. There is nothing I want that is materialistic that I would dedicate my life to; but I think that the world expects me to work toward something.

When someone asks, "What do you want?" "To be happy" seems to be an insufficient answer for them. Why should "happy" be the wrong answer? Is it not possible to live for what I feel?

At times I feel that I need something materialistic from the world. I know it's wrong to steal or to expect someone else to provide it for me. Therefore, I work a job. I don't live for that job, but rather use that job to sustain myself.

At times I feel that no one understands me; perhaps because most of the time I don't understand myself. Maybe I do understand myself but what I understand goes against what others say is right. It seems that when I think of only what I want that I feel guilty because the world says, "It's wrong to think only of what I want."

The feelings I experience when I help someone in trouble is inexplicable, yet so great. The feeling I get from someone who is ungrateful is maddening and I swear not to help again. But, I know I will.

Does life have a direction? Must we really have a goal of some kind? Is "to be happy" really a goal? It doesn't seem right just to exist. But that is what I've done until now. I have no true direction. Is this a weakness or something that must be? Must I make some choice, take some stand?

Is it really possible that God wants me? If He does want me what does He want me to do? Does He want me to open my heart to the world? Does He want me to speak His word? Or to write what I feel to help others just feel?

Is there too much concern in the world for things and not enough for people? Do things just happen or are they all a part of His plan? What is His plan? How can one be sure?

Am I a phony? Do I say things because I know people want to hear them? NO! At least of that one thing I am sure. I say what I feel, and saying what I feel has got to be good, even if there are consequences for being so revealing of my imperfections.

(Circa 1970, in my prodigal years)

WHERE DO I GO?

Where do I go
when I stare out there?
Where do I go?

What is it at which I stare,
while looking perfectly happy to be there?

Where I have been
I may never know,
for no memory
comes with me,
when from this peaceful place
I am forced to leave.

To NOW it is
that I return
and for a place I know not of
I yearn.
As the feeling slowly leaves me
and to this life I return

Just before I let it go
someone may say

"I want to share
that peaceful place
at which you stare."

But there is no way
I can take anyone there
For I too ask,
where do I go
when I stare out there?

WHERE ARE YOU GOD?

Where are you, God?
Are you one of my inner voices?
Are you the voice of guilt trips,
the voice of justification,
the voice of fear and love,
or are you the voice which
calmly sorts things out?

Where are you, God?
Are you my vision when I feel
unlimited in awareness,
my hearing when sorrows only
whispered are heard,
my feelings when emotions
around me are absorbed?

Are You a part of me at all
or I a part of You?

I was created solely "me"
but am I now
a part of the Three
or are You all a part of me?

Where are you, God?

circa 1970

MY SOUL

What do you look like?
Created in the image of God I'm told.
But what do you look like?

This earth suit is not the image of God.
This body is skin, bones, and chemicals,
it will not live on for eternity
but my soul, you will.

It is you
that has the relationship with God
It is you
He speaks to
so how do I connect with you?

I want to hear Him in my mind or heart.

You are the part of me
that will live forever!
How do I connect with you?
What do you look like?

HOW?

How do you explain
walking in the rain, flying in a plane,
the feeling of pain? How do you explain?

How do you tell feeling so well,
having been through hell,
a strange smell? How do you tell?

How do you share
the clean fresh air, showing you care,
having been there? How do you share?

How do you express
the sun's caress, being penniless
feeling youthfulness? How do you express?

How do you word watching the flight of a bird,
the strangest sound you've ever heard?
How do you word?

How do you show?
watching a child grow, a waterfall flow,
feeling slow? How do you show?

How do you communicate
loving to skate, being the only one late,
hate? How do you communicate?

How do you convey a farmer's pride harvesting hay,
having to go away, falling in love the first day?
How do you convey?

How do you expose
the beauty of a rose
or any of those?

1975 Atlanta, Georgia

DON'T DOUBT ME

Why do you look at me
the way you do?
Is it too unbelievable that
I can be true?

What must I do?
What must I say
for you to know
I'm really this way?

I've asked myself,
of this you may be sure,
If the words I speak
are the truths I seek.

The answer comes
as if from another mind,

"Doubt not yourself, for you are
true and kind,
and of those that doubt you,
pay no mind."

Yet I ask you,
why do you look at me
the way you do?
Can you not simply accept
my kindness to you?

BAR RAP

Are you really who you say you are?
Or did you make yourself up
on the way here in your car?

Tell me no lies,
for I have heard them all,
give me the truth and we can both stand tall

If we grow together
on a foundation of lies,
there will always be doubt in each other's eyes

So come what may
no matter what happens
start today while our relationship
is in its youth. Speak to me only the truth!

COINCIDENCE OR FATE?

Why did we meet?
Why did we meet?
The answer to that question
is not yet complete.

Was it by fate?
Will we find the answer
before it's too late?

Too late for what?
Are we meant for friendship,
or are we meant for hate?
I hope it's friendship,
I hate hate!

For my friend and typist Connie B (J)

THOUGHTS
OF
GOD

SEARCH

I searched for God at the shore of the sea
but His presence was hidden from me.
I could really see that the ocean was His
but it was obvious that was not where He lives.

I sought to find Him in the blue skies above
but while they were pretty, I could not feel His love.
oh, I could see that they were painted by Him
but I could not find Him dwelling within.

I walked in the woods among the trees and the birds
but still not a sound from Him could be heard.
There was no doubt that this was His creation
but it was not the place of His habitation.

I looked to the night sky full to the brim
but still it gave me no direction to Him.
the jewels above were surely His own
but it was clear this was not His home.

I began to think we would always remain apart
then someone shared how to have Him in my heart.
Someone told me about Calvary
and how this Messiah Jesus died for me.

I fell to my knees and called out His name.
He came to me and washed away my shame.
Now I no longer search for Him
for now at last, He dwells within.

JESUS, I AM A JEW!

My Mother told me
"We don't believe in you,
for if I did, I'd no longer be a Jew!"
Now what am I supposed to do?
For I believe! Why, I even pray to you!
And you know what Yeshua?
I'm still a Jew!
Just, my Messiah, the same as You!

I LIVE!

You say that I'm not real. You say I'm someone's dream.
But when I get a hold of you
You'll scream, you'll scream, you'll scream!

I've planned it very carefully, using your natural gifts.
Using your very mind. You think I don't exist.
You think that I'm a joke. But when I get a hold of you
You'll wish you carried His yoke

You see me in a silly red suit with funny little horns on my head
But you'll know I'm much more than that
when finally you are dead

You'll find I've been a woman. You'll find I've been a man.
You'll find I've been what I had to be and
everything you thought I couldn't do
You'll know, I can, I can, I can!

There is nothing that can keep you from me except, of course, that
Jesus. But if you don't believe in me and I'm everywhere to see.
Then it's logical to think You'll never escape from me.

If you don't believe in me,
I don't give it a thought,
so long as you don't carry His yoke
and follow what He has taught.

You say that I'm not real. You say I'm someone's dream
But when I get a hold of you
you'll scream, you'll scream, you'll scream!

Charlotte, North Carolina 1980 for a Youth For Christ group

I HAVE BEEN A SERVANT TO SIN

I have been a servant to sin,
often willingly, sometimes unconsciously.
Now in agony.

Through prayer, I break the bonds of habit,
and through the Word, I become a servant to Jesus.

I have been a servant to sin,
locked in a lifestyle of choices made by emotion,
choices which weren't for my best.

But the wide curving pathway of past decisions was deeply dug.
 I simply followed the rut.

I have been a servant to sin.
My rewards felt good for a season.
But, the season was always short.
Now I walk along the narrow path.
I am a servant to Him Who walked this road before me

My choices are now made with open heart and mind.
I enjoy the rewards which do not quickly end.
Peace in my soul replaces being driven in my flesh.
Contentment replaces the elusive chase for pleasure.

I am a servant to Jesus. But, the truth is, I am free.
And I'd rather be with Him, than to be a servant to sin

Lausanne, Switzerland 1990 - Romans 6:16-18 John 8:34-26

THE SIMPLE LIFE

In six days He did the deed,
working out of joy, not out of need.

A place in the sun was the way it was begun,
just a man and a woman and a world of fun.
To eat and to drink, to love and to pray,
Oh, doesn't it sound like a wonderful
way to spend the day?

What would you think that we must do
for the right to live this way?
Would you believe, just one simple rule
is all we must obey?

From the tree of knowledge,
 the fruit we must not eat.
Such a simple rule we did not keep.

The serpent came and deceived us one night.
From the forbidden fruit he lured us to bite,
From that moment on, we've known wrong from right.
We moved into darkness and lost His light.

On our own, we drifted about.
Filled with sadness, filled with doubt,
We built a world from God apart,
yet longing to have Him in our heart.

We now ache for what was meant to be
for the simple life beneath that tree,
Walking in the garden, hearing His voice
as if we'd never made that terrible choice.

LIFE STAGES OF MY MESSIAH

You were a baby; crawling, gurgling, drooling,
the Creator of sound itself unable to utter a word.

You were a toddler; learning to walk, touching everything You
could, experiencing with human hands all that You created.

You were a teenager; what a sight You must have been sitting there
with the Rabbis talking about the words You wrote.

You were a man; working in the carpenter shop with dad, making
chairs, tables, cabinets. Then suddenly, You put down your tools,
kissed mother good-bye and walked to the Jordan, where John
baptized You, and Father affirmed Your call.

You were a Rabbi; at thirty, a teacher, a healer, a lover of the
unlovable, calling those whom You created to walk with
God the Father in a relationship rather than a rulebook.

You were obedient; fulfilling the scripture You wrote, not uttering
a word as they shed Your blood. Then, at the end, it was not man's
"I'll get even, but Father, forgive them."

You were dead; they pulled Your limp body from the cross.
How frail you seemed. Only three hours, so little time to kill the
Greatest Man to ever live. Filled with tears and not understanding,
those who loved You, carried You to the tomb.

You didn't stay there! You conquered death! Three hours to die,
three days dead and then victory!
You returned, bringing us the gift of eternity.

You live, high and lifted up, at the Father's side and in the hearts
of all of us who believe.
You are My Messiah!

2008 Atlanta, Georgia

MY KING LIVES

My King left His throne, born into the human race as a baby, crawling, gurgling, drooling; the Creator of sound unable to utter a word.

My King grew into an uncrowned royal toddler, learning to walk, touching everything around Him, experiencing, with human hands, all that He created.

My King, unrecognized, grew into a Jewish teenager, talking with the Temple Rabbis who marveled at His words, not grasping His royalty or the fact that their Messiah was enlightening for them the very words He wrote.

My King grew into manhood working in the carpenter shop with His earthly Abba making chairs, tables, cabinets. Then suddenly, His Highness put down the tools, kissed His mother good-bye and walked to the Jordan where John recognized His Royalty and baptized Him, and Father affirmed His call.

My King, knowing this earth was not His kingdom, served as a Rabbi at thirty, a teacher, a healer, a lover of the unlovable, calling those whom He created to walk with God the Father in relationship rather than a rulebook.

My King was obedient to His earthly call as completely God and completely man, fulfilling the scripture He wrote, not uttering a word as they shed His Royal blood. On the cross, it was not revenge but "Father, forgive them." "King of the Jews" scornfully tacked on His cross.

My King died! Soldiers pulled His limp body from the cross. How frail He seemed! Only three hours, so little time to kill the greatest Man to ever live. Overcome with tears, not understanding, those who loved my King carried Him the tomb.

My King did not remain in the tomb. He conquered death. Three hours to die, three days dead, and then victory! The King of the Jews became the King for all humankind giving us the gift of eternity.

My King now lives high and lifted up at the Father's side and in the hearts of all of us who believe.
My King Lives!
Is your King alive?

with Arlene Samuels 2010 Atlanta, Georgia

GOOD SHABBAT

Bricks and mortar, beams and trusses, nails and screws, wood and sheetrock, paint and plaster, chandeliers and painted glass a building, but not an ordinary one. A single large room, glowing white, long sleek seats, and a balcony above

A gathering place for people with a purpose, not a grand theatre with actors on the screen, but rather a stage, with sacred performers for an audience of One

God looks down, a smile of pleasure on His face. "It's Shabbat," He says to an audience of Angels. "See, My people remember. They gather before Me again. It's not quite time but now they gather and settle in. Look, the children laugh and play in the pews, the mothers greet and smile, all understanding each other's process to settle the children down."

"They are here, from newborn to almost with Me, a simple chant, a call to the Shema, I love their song. I love their prayers, the prayers of my people. Yes, My chosen ones remembering Me!"

"See the Torah scrolls how carefully they handle them, as if they were carrying Me in their arms. I feel their love, their commitment –it's so good. And each week on Shabbat it does not get old."

"The prayers, the silent sitting in My presence, the cares of the week slipping away as they enter My rest. They need this- I love giving it to them-My rest. My people-My chosen people. The scrolls come down the aisle back to shelter. My people reach out and kiss and carefully, softly touch. They don't know I feel the kisses and relish their touch. Final smiles-prayers and praises."

"Hugs and chatter, now "good Shabbats" all around. Yes, it is good and now food will follow. Their spirits are calm, their appetites awake. My people are in My rest…Good Shabbat"

Atlanta GA October 9, 2006

ONLY HE KNOWS

I came here this morning just before dawn
to sit quietly in the park.
The sounds of people usually about
were nowhere to be heard.

The only sound that broke the quiet
was the chirping of a bird.

Surrounded by the works of God
I sat beneath a tree and the hassles of
everyday life no longer affected me
for I let my mind go free.

There was no decision that I came to make
only of peace and quiet did I wish to partake.

Sitting there beneath that tree
I felt His presence near to me.
"My Lord," I said, "Are you here with me?"
And the first ray of the sun broke through the trees

The sounds of birds were suddenly there
and hundreds of them filled the air.

What was left of the dark was consumed by the light.
My soul felt as if it too was taking flight.

TRUST

Trust
is an easy word to say
but it's hard to abide in
day by day

Trust
It's a word which implies peace
a lasting, deep abiding state
which does not cease

Trust
Oh, Lord, I do with my soul
but in daily living
my trust has a hole

Trust
I seem to rely on my occupation
my bankbook and other plans
not the peace of Your salvation

Trust
I had it once when first we met
but day by day
I've allowed myself to forget

Trust
Dear Lord, all depends on You
help me Lord to cling again
and live my life as I'm to do

Trusting
Trusting
Lord, in You

Hilton Head Island October 31, 1981

GOD IS WITHIN

You're not claiming any longer that Christianity is for you.
You say now that no organized religion will do.
You once called out His name and asked Him to
remove your shame, but now you question, Is God alive or is He
dead? Was He here to begin with? Perhaps He is just a myth.

Look about you, here and there, the work of God is everywhere.
Look back to your heart, for here you will find that God is still a part.
Remember the times before you let His joy slip away, when you
sought His fellowship night and day. Think of the times your heart
went out to others, the times they felt like your sisters and brothers.

Think of the times you knew others were sad. Surely you remember
that you felt bad, and how you'd pray and watch them become glad
It's times like these when you really care
that God's presence within, you must know is still there.

WHEREVER YOU SHALL BE

Where ever you seek Me, alone or gathered in My name
I have said I shall be, and so every Tuesday morning
finds Me at the sea where the brotherhood of Hilton Head
rises early from their beds for breakfast with each other and Me.

Men from many walks who have listened to My talks and gathered
unto Me in common unity, there on Tuesday morning also shall I be
to hear their words of prayer and share their common bond,
love for the Father, the fellowship of the Spirit, and wanting time
with Me. And so as I have promised there shall I be

Hilton Head Island, South Carolina 1983

28

CHRISTIAN SNOB

Christian snob,
staunch and rigid,
with your Bible in
your hands
and self
righteousness
in your heart

Quoting your rules,
and regulations
as the proper
and only acceptable
Christian behavior

So blinded by the
black and white
you see no room
for gray.

And in your snobbishness
you've forgotten or
perhaps never learned
that the only rule
that really counts
is that we love God,
the Lord Jesus
and each other.

LEAD ME TO HIM (Based on Luke 18-15 & 16)

Dedicated to all Sunday School Teachers and Children's Pastors!

Our parents brought us to Him to be hugged
But His disciples tried to stop us.
The Lord said, "Let them come to Me".
He even said, "You are the Kingdom of God."

From that time on His disciples brought us to Him
Wherever He went, His disciples called to our parents
"Bring your children now to see the Lord."
And He hugged each and every one of us.

Oh His touch! It was like nothing else.
We were so free and open to receive it.
We were protected by the disciples.
No one in the crowds could stop us.

Now the times have changed.
His disciples have all gone home with Him,
And there is an enemy working daily to distract us.
Lack of opportunity has decreased our desire to know Him

However, some of us have been praying since we heard about you
We hear you are His modern disciples and you care about us.
They tell us you will part the crowds for us
That you will chase away the distractions

Is it true that you have created some fun ways,
that will help us to learn about Him?
Is it true that you give up your time to be His new disciples
and once again make a way through the crowd?

We talk often about what the Lord said,
that we are the kingdom of God.
We have so much to learn and grow
Thank you for loving us and teaching us what we must know.

IT'S NOT JUST A DIP IN THE WATER

It's not just a dip in the water
It's a dying and living again
It's a sign, a step of faith
It's a step of obedience, a divine order

When we are gently put under
and all of our flesh covered over,
there is a mysterious washing-away
of forever putting our sins asunder.

When we arise again from the deep
into the Holy Spirit hovering over,
we are enveloped into the presence of God.

So significant and powerful is this obedience
that in nations where freedom does not rule
and the enemy of our souls has his guards
it can bring about untold severe consequences.

Yes, the enemy does not see this as just a dip in the water.
He knows we have made a choice against him.
He knows he has lost control of our souls forever.
He hates that we've chosen obedience to a divine order

But here in the Land of the Free, we arise to serve
without fear dealing only with the battle of temptation and
the intolerance of non believers.

It's not just a dip in the water.
It's our declaration of freedom from sin.
It's the first step in walking with Him.
And it's for all who want to begin.

Roswell, Georgia October 28, 2007

REFLECTIONS
ON
FAMILY AND FRIENDS

MY SLEEPING CHILD

My sleeping child, you will never know
how many times I look upon your face,
gently stroke your tender cheeks,
lightly brush aside the hair from your face.

Reliving precious memories of our days,
knowing all too fully how time slips away.
Seems like just a short while ago,
I held you for the first time.

Now we're up to band-aids for sores that aren't there,
imaginary friends who go with you everywhere,
Spiderman--Superman—and Wonder Woman, too,
are all important people and very real to you.

You dress yourself—even pick out your clothes
and dictate your very own special breakfast treat.
You play away your day with the energy of two
and bedtime is the very worst thing to happen to you.

My sleeping child, you will never know
of my tender kisses in the night
my chest filling with pride
Until, my sleeping child, you sit beside
a sleeping child of your own

1975 Atlanta, Georgia

MILESTONE

Today marks a milestone you did nothing to achieve,
it's a day to leave childhood behind but not a day to grieve.
What lies ahead is like no other freedom God has given
it's the right to choose your own way of living.

Today I call you a man, my son;
not fully an adult as society defines it,
but in our Jewish culture a man nonetheless.

At this age in Jewish custom
you become accountable for yourself and your actions.
In ancient history there were responsibilities galore
no longer considered a child as before.

While those choices are not options for today,
there are choices you must make in the very same way.

You must stand now on your own
in being accountable before God's throne.
You can fall on your knees or ball up your fist
it's a decision no man is allowed to resist.

You have chosen to serve our Jesus, also a Jew.
You have asked the God of Mom & Dad to be the God over
you. We call His name Yeshua, for He is our Messiah.
Now let Him be the center of all that you desire.

This is the most important choice you'll ever make;
Though there will be many other decisions for you to take.
I'm proud to present you with this Tallith my son;
for every Jewish praying man should have one.

I bless you in Yeshua's name. I call you son.
I call you man. Most important of all,
I call you man of God! I love you, Chad!

For Chad, 2002, Mt. Pleasant, SC

A GIFT OF LIFE AND LOVE FROM ROMANIA

You were born in 1991, a fine April day
unaware that we were coming to take you away
Years before, we began praying for you
not knowing who you were, or what we should do

You were born to a young woman who lived in despair
but knowing she wanted to get you out of there.
She was full of love for you, she too not knowing what to do.

Her great gift was giving life to you
and for twenty-eight days she did the best she could do
Then she wrapped you in tiny borrowed clothes of white
and started off to Arad in the dark of night

In a smoke filled court house, she found your new mother
as she looked into the smiling face of your big brother.
A mother and father, and a big brother too
she knew sending you to America was the best for you

Just imagine the scene that miraculous day
Two mothers crying, as we gently carried you away.
One mother's tears of joy to adopt her tiny little girl
The other knowing she'd done right to give her the world

Whether birth mother or not, our children are on loan
They belong to God until He takes them home.
Your mother and I and big brother Chad too
are ever so grateful that God gave us you.
 We love you Gloria Grace!

1991 Arad, Romania, in honor of Gloria Grace's Adoption

I WONDER IF YOU'LL REMEMBER

I wonder if you'll remember
the times we stayed in bed and played
and played and played and played
when your giggles filled the room

I wonder if you'll remember
the walking and talking
when you just listened to my voice
and smiled at every word

I wonder if you'll remember
being thrown into the air
putting your little shoes into my big pair
and walking around with a grin

I wonder if you'll remember
ABC cards, speedy little cars,
building blocks, your stuffed zoo,
picture books, and cuckoo clocks
each producing their own special smile
from you.

I wonder if you'll remember
all the cities & countries we traveled through
always managing to find something special for you
and everything igniting a smile and a laugh

I wonder if you'll remember
but I know I always will

April 22, 1990 Lausanne, Switzerland for Chad

PARENT TO PERSON

I see you as you are
grown though you may be
but you'll always be my child
within my memory

Although I find at times,
it's hard to communicate
let me share these words
before it's too late

For your precious life
you owe nothing to me
as that was given to you
by the Lord of eternity

You owe me nothing
that I don't earn
yet as your parent
your love and respect I yearn

Please don't feel as though
my desires you must fulfill
for you have your own life to live
this is within God's will

I simply want to take the time
to make this understood
of all the things within my life
that caused me to feel good

Nothing is more rewarding
then you and parenthood!

APART

You couldn't fall asleep in my arms like other children do.
I wasn't there to help you with what you learned in school.

There were many days when by your side you wanted me
and I guess it seemed to you there was someplace else I'd rather be.

Sometimes when we make a choice we don't get all we want.
If it could've been a reality you'd have spent more time with me.

When two people get a divorce no matter who's at fault or even if
there's none, it's still the child who loses out on days of love and fun

Many days I do recall the aches and pains within from wanting
just to hold you like I had before.

I'd even considered going back and living a lie for you. But I knew
that just couldn't and wouldn't do.

Now the years have passed. Both of us now know that I chose the
only way I felt was right to go.

Here we are two adults with decisions we must choose
we have a chance to catch up on the love we both had to lose.

Come try to understand me, let me learn of you
let us share together the love we are both due.

FAMILY APART

Our family like a tree has many branches growing free.
Some are strong; some are weak and like the tree we don't speak.

There are times when I'd like to call, to hear their voices;
to love them all. But I don't call, neither do they,
we all put it off till another day.

I have family less close than friends; I wonder how our relationship
will end. There was once or twice that we were close, but now we're
further apart than most.

I miss not having a family, but maybe this is how it must be,
for they must be themselves and I must be me.

FAMILY IN BLOOM

Our family like a tree has many branches growing free
some are strong, others are weak but unlike the tree we do speak

There are times when we are in full bloom and share close harmony
There are times when we are bare and scattered everywhere

and like the tree we have our roots buried deep within
an ever present memory that indeed we are still a family

TODAY IS MY CHILD'S WEDDING DAY

Today is my child's wedding day.
Seems like only yesterday
my wife and I exchanged our vows,
dashing off as bride and groom
with our new love full in bloom

Today is my child's wedding day.
I can't seem to stop the tears from rolling
Tears of joy, which keep on flowing.

Today is my child's wedding day.
It's a long way from formulas and diapers,
late night feedings – bedtime readings
and disputes with other boys and girls brewing

Today is my child's wedding day.
I watch as on bended knees they began to pray
and as I listened, I heard them say
"I give myself to you today."

Two I do's and an I pronounce,
handshakes and kisses, smiles and best wishes.
a handsome groom and a beautiful bride
my chest bursting with joy and pride.

Today is my child's wedding day.

ACQUAINTANCE

Life's crossings
are anywhere
anytime.

I want as many
crossings as possible
to be peaceful.

If I am as welcome
in your world
as you are in mine,
perhaps the future
will find us close;
perhaps not.

In any event,
our crossing has
been peaceful,
and you will
be remembered!

For my friend Linda W (Modine)

PROBLEMS AND FREEDOMS: YOURS, MINE, AND OTHERS

CITY MIDNIGHT

I walk the streets of the city
the midnight people
filling each doorway
with potential danger
imagined,
possible,
probable,
but this night, avoided.

The city:
concrete, asphalt, bright lights
disappointed yesterdays,
unplanned tomorrows,
dollars and survival the topic
of each new day.

The city:
where privacy is a premium
friendships are numbered,
and space is something
rockets get launched into.

NYC circa 1986

FREEDOM 1996

It was 1776
people were hurt by far more than sticks.
scars of battle were everywhere,
but there was new hope rising in the air.
Young and old fought day and night
to win our freedom we now consider a right.

Yes, it was more than 200 years ago today
Wow! We've come a long, long way!
We are freer now than we've ever been...
all of us...regardless of the color of our skin.
The people that rule are still a chosen few,
but now they are chosen by me and by you.

We are free now to ask far more than, "Why?"
and we can ask our "Why?" aloud,
without fear of bullets fired blindly into the crowd.

We are free to go our own way,
free to choose where we will stay,
free to choose how or if to pray.

Things may not be perfect as they are today.
but all things considered,
individual freedom's come a long, long way

July 4th 1996 for those who gave the ultimate

BLACK BICENTENNIAL

Yes you are black
and for almost 200 years
the man's been on your back.

You've walked in the gutter,
rode the back of the bus.
You've been called nigger
and were afraid to make a fuss.

Ah, but the times have changed.
Equality is being rearranged.
We are singing songs of a different tune.
We are singing songs of freedom's bloom.

Getting this freedom
has been no easy thing.
Remember the marches led
by Dr. Martin Luther King?

He and others paved the way
to bring freedom to
where it is today.
Don't let their memory slip away

Many people of all colors and race
are working today to fulfill the dream
to make freedom in America
the best for all we've ever seen.

Atlanta, Georgia 1976

DAWN IN THE WOODS

I stood this morning at the top of a hill,
and the world in all its beauty was still.
There were trees ever so green
spread as far as could be seen,
and my sight as I looked about
became ever so keen.

I saw birds and squirrels, rabbit and deer.
I even thought I'd seen a bear.
Oh Lord, it's nice to be here
enjoying life without a care
breathing this beautiful clean fresh air.

There was a brook running nearby
and I sipped its water beneath a clear blue sky
enjoying a very natural "high."
I listened closely to the sounds I heard
especially those of a nearby bird.
Its sound was as pleasant as could be
its song set my mind free.

I felt an inner peace come to me.
My chest rose and fell in a even smooth stride
enjoying nature's beauty
with eyes open wide.

As the sun slowly lost its glow,
it came to me that I must go.
I'd lingered longer than I should
but I took with me memories full of good.

HOOKED

In the morning before getting on your clothes
you reach out to light up one of those

So round, So firm, So fully packed
It's a heavy monkey on your back

Your teeth get yellow, your breath is stale
But all you can think about is to inhale

Running and playing you can't get far
Maybe you'll try one that has less tar.

After a meal you've got to have it
Has it become more than a habit?

Pack after pack you throw them away
Only to buy more the very same day

I'll quit tomorrow you tell yourself
Yes, that's the one, Miss, right there on the shelf

You put out the light and go to bed
Cigarette smoke circling 'round your head

You're Hooked!

In the 1970's the American Cancer Society of Georgia
used my poem for their smoking awareness program.

BE REAL

All around we can hear the cry,
Who am I? Who am I?
So many people search for the answer
until the day they die.

So many people come and go,
never learning what they must know.
What am I meant for? What shall I do?
God dear God, If only I knew.

Some search to identify with someone else,
never having the courage to look to themselves.
They aimlessly search, their minds in a spin
for the answer that lies only within.

For some it is easy to run away,
they haven't the courage to face the next day.
For some it is easy to face the next day,
they haven't the courage to turn away.

All around we can hear the cry.
Who am I? Who am I?
So many search for the answer
until the day they die.

And yet the answer is as clear as day and night.
You must do what together with God
helps you know you're right.
Be Real, Above all, be real!

METAMORPHOSIS

The caterpillar climbs a tree and finds
What it considers an appropriate place;
It creates a cocoon, a safe haven
For the process of re-birth.
Somehow, without dying
It ceases to be what it once was.

Perhaps the process is without pain.
No one really knows except the caterpillar.
And those memories stay in the cocoon,
for the butterfly moves too freely
to carry a burden of any sort

But what of me? What of man?
How do I find a safe haven for this process
of rebirth occurring within me?

Surely, I'm not dying
It just feels that way as old patterns of survival
are revealed to be trails to destruction of relationships
which count and cannot take the strain

But, I cannot climb. There is no cocoon!
The process isn't hidden and there is pain.

This pain cuts deep within. It reveals memories
of past ways and shames. Yet there is hope.
Because the surgery in process
is being performed by the Spirit of God

Who has the power to heal in such a way
so that as time passes, I too, can leave behind
those burdens too heavy to carry, in a cocoon,
I cannot see and move along
As the butterfly- FREE!

New York City 1986

BEAUTIFUL DAY

Shrimp boats are floating lazily
on the magic of glistening ocean.
The waves are flowing gently
to the shore.
I am aglow from the sun's caress.
I am alone…I am at peace.

I have watched the sunrise come
awed by its splendor.
I have watched the flight of seagulls
as they glided across a fiery sky.

I have experienced the tide changing
and the ocean giving birth
to the shore

I've seen early morning strollers
gathering up the shells, lovers cycling,
leaving trails to be erased by the next tide.

I've been amazed by the gracefulness
of Border Collies and German Shepherds
leaping across the shore line

I've had a beautiful day,
and it has only just begun.

South Carolina Coast:
for our two wonderful departed loyal dogs, Moondance, our German Shepherd
and Oliver, our Border Collie

A SOUTHERN RIDE TO YESTERDAY

Southern two-lane road, peaceful as can be,
laid so very carefully, to save every possible tree.
People fishing from a wooden bridge, happy as can be,
not a single look of frustration on their faces can I see.

I'm on a Low-Country ride to yesterday and everywhere I see,
just another sign, of another time, that keeps on calling to me,
a time of peace when all seemed well
a time, a time of the southern belle

There's grand old houses standing tall, with rockers leaning
against the wall, retaining all of their beauty still, as if possessed
by their builders' will.

The songs of birds and a gentle breeze
fill the mighty old oak trees, which, if they could,
surely would make yesterday understood.

I'm on a Low-Country ride to yesterday and everywhere I see
just another sign, of another time, that keeps on calling to me,
a time of peace when all seemed well
a time, a time of the southern belle

Clear blue skies and the setting sun
sailboats making their final run
the ocean coming to the shore, as it always has before.

They're all memories of yesterday, here today,
meant always to stay, within the view of the very few
who take the time to see.

I'm on a Low-Country ride to yesterday
and everywhere I see just another sign of another time,
that keeps on calling to me, that keeps on calling to me.

South Carolina, en route to Hilton Head Island 1977

PANHANDLER ON SATURDAY MORNING

He's 6 feet four at least. Still wiry and able to move about swiftly.
Years ago he was probably an all star on
his high school basketball team

But the crowds are gone-the cheers only foggy memories
which he recalls whenever he passes a store window
that has a TV showing a basketball game.

He staggers, in a reality of his own, with palm outstretched,
from person to person, receiving not a cent.
At Fifty First and Fifth, he corners two women
overdressed for the morning, waiting for the traffic light to change.

He shows them his longest saddest face, with palm shakily
outstretched, mumbling about his need

One stares at the traffic light, as if her eyes could somehow make it
move swiftly through its cycle. The other stares at him
her eyes cold and her head moving firmly from side to side.

Finally green - and WALK! - They move on.
He stands there watching as they cross the street,
scratching his head, wondering how they could have
resisted his best lines.

Suddenly he shrugged his shoulders,
turns and in the early morning daylight
urinates on The Bank Of Ireland.

New York City May, 25 1986

TWO VIEWS FROM THE FOOT OF
THE FIFTY NINTH STREET BRIDGE

She is elegant in her long flowing gown,
an appropriate color for royalty...purple.
Silver haired, survivor of many years in
a man's world, back before "the changes."
She too has come "a long way, baby."

On the ground floor of a high rise, high priced,
Fifty Ninth Street East.
Sitting at a fine wood table in front of the window
daintily eating wheat toast & strawberries, drinking coffee
and wondering if she had room for
orange juice.

Glancing through her Wall Street Journal,
She is oblivious of me at the foot of the bridge,
or the woman below the bridge,
who came a long way on another road
now encamped in a cardboard box,
with all her belongings in a shopping cart.

Robed in rags, too dirty to tell their color,
her hair, also silver, but not quite so bright,
Sitting on the concrete
leaning against a wire mesh fence,
scavenging through some food scraps
which she lifted out of a deli garbage can,

muttering something about
giving her right arm for
a glass of
orange juice

New York City May 25, 1986

53

ANOTHER POET IS DEAD

Today another poet is dead
and the world may never
know his name.
Today another man has
returned from whence he came.

My friend Jim Jackson
is in your presence Lord.
He needs no words
of prayer from me,
bid him "hello" my Lord

Now those of us he left behind
we ask, my Lord, Be kind.
Help us forget any memories of
Jim's pain, help us smile
at the mention of his name

Grant to us the strength
to find the peace that lies
beneath our own pain
of a love we will miss
again and again

And help us, Lord
to remember Jim's goal was the spreading
of Your kingdom through his words
and his actions.
for the glory of Your Name.

For my friend Jim Jackson
Hilton Head Island, SC Gone Home June 2, 1977

SYMPATHY

Death has taken
someone you love.
Cry your tears,
Feel your pain,
then pick up
the pieces
and start to live
your life again...

...Keeping the memory
of your loved one alive
and always a part of you

PEOPLE DIE

Only God knows
why and when people die

But when
in His wisdom
He chooses
our loved ones
to return home
to Him
let us rejoice
for their
good fortune

LIVING WITH BI-POLAR

My eyes open, daylight surrounds my body, but my mind is in darkness. My emotions, my spirit, my will are all enveloped in darkness. It is a strange darkness but I am not a stranger to it. I start most days here. I am closed in, cannot, will not, and don't even want to try to escape this darkness. My only regret in these moments is that I can feel it and I want only not to. I feel that I am in a coffin deep underground and the daylight cannot reach me.

My physical self arises reluctantly, climbs into clothing, and tries to kick start the day. I hear my soul mate attempt to reassure me as we take our morning walk. "You can't help that you are bi-polar. Let's look at the positive in our lives." We talk about being able to walk, not having physical pain, the highlights of our life, her gratefulness for our years of marriage and her appreciation of my companionship. My spirit begins to lift but is unable to push through the lid of the coffin.

"Help me," my spirit cries out to awaken my will, "Help me out of here!" Without thinking, acting in response to the cry, my will pushes the coffin top off. The flow of dirt surrounds me, emotions cry out, "Leave me alone! Let me be!" Holding my hand, my love leads me in a little song I wrote long ago. "In the name of Jesus, I declare that I am free. In the name of Jesus, there are no holds on me, I am free, I am free, I am free." I join her and we sing it over and over until I feel my will say "no" to emotions.

Will begins the climb, digging up, spirit joins in the song, & emotions want no part of it. Breaking to the surface, will decides to go for the day, spirit is smiling and soaring. Emotions want to crawl back in the hole, cover up and just be left alone. I will myself into activity. I force my emotions to pay attention to "It's not about me." Emotions scream out "It is! It is! It is about me. I have no reason to enter this day." But will and Spirit continue on until emotions either join in or just quietly endure. And I am free to live another day in the sunshine of life.

That is what it was like before proper diagnosis and medication. I encourage you, if your day begins anything like mine did, get treatment and freedom!

A CHAT WITH AN EXISTER

He was 67, retired now,
"A railroad man" he said
As he scratched his tan bald head.

We sat on a bench and watched his dog play.
He said "This is the way I spend my day,
just passing the time away"

I asked, "Is there nothing else you want to do?"
When he gave me his answer
I almost cried.

There were no people he wanted to see,
Nowhere else he wanted to be
And it was too painful
To bring back any memory.

He never liked to read,
"It is a bore!" he said
As again he scratched his head.

He's lived his whole senior life
Just passing the time away.

He will leave this world without anyone having
the slightest trace of his doing so.

What bothers me most
Is that he doesn't
 even care.

ODE TO THE BOTTLE

Little bottles full drink,
you had far more power than I did think.
To please you I gave up my very life just for the next drink

But your demands grew even stronger
and rather than lose you, I gave up school and worked no longer.

So there we were, the two of us, and still for you
this was not enough.

There was complete alienation, from friends and family
and even jail. You carried me to the depths of hell,
and even then I didn't rebel.

All these things for the pleasure of you
and only now have I realized taking my life
is what you were trying to do.

But I am fighting you no longer alone.
I have my higher power (God) to help me home.
The people that I hurt are also here
I don't understand why, but they still care

Sober now, I have a program to work,
I'm no longer a jerk.
The rest of my life I choose to be free
of your enticing memory.

Bottle be gone from me for you again I never want to see.

(1978 Through the eyes of a friend)

Sometimes when we write on a subject, others see far deeper than we did. Below is a great example.

THE BATTLE FOR PROGRESS

A chain saw screams as its inhuman teeth tear deep
into the very being of an a supposedly unfeeling tree

A bulldozer pushes against the same unyielding tree
roaring in unison with the chain saw toward their goal
destruction in the name of progress
Screaming , pushing , cutting, pushing and suddenly
the agony of being splintered, scattered everywhere.

The cracking and ripping sounds fill the air as at last
being able to resist no longer
a supposedly unfeeling tree succumbs
Its remains are pushed across the road
in victory-dance fashion and progress continues

THE BATTLE FOR LIFE (RN Martha Sears' insight)

A suction tip or scalpel intrudes
as it tears deep into a supposedly unfeeling embryo
the sterile instrument scrapes
and pushes against tenacious tissue
as suction is turned on

Destruction in the name of convenience
scraping, sucking continue
the agony of being torn scattered
while the splattering sounds fill the room

At last being able to resist no longer
a supposedly unfeeling human being succumbs
His/Her remains are sent to the lab in lieu of a funeral
and the victor goes home

circa 1978 Hilton Head Island, SC

59

I am often asked, "When did you start writing poetry?" I started to keep the panic down and my sanity intact during a dramatic experience. The result was ...

BIG RIG IN THE DIG

I was driving in the rain, in control, I made the turn, my rear end skids. I fight to right it but continue to slide. Sureness is gone, panic is near, and suddenly I'm leaning left. Totally still for a few seconds and then over I go, I roll. No one is around to see the rig go and I cannot help but wonder who will know.

I open my eyes; I'm all alone, thanking God I'll get to go home. The longest climb I now begin to fight my way out of this hunk of iron and tin. My feet reach the ground, I stumble away, and I say to myself this is my last day. I handle the phone calls still unaware that tomorrow again I will dare.

The king of the road once mighty and strong is lying there now where it doesn't belong. It's only a machine I tell myself, yet I can't help but feel it's all by itself. Grunting and groaning, I seem to imagine as if it were saying, "How could this happen?

The tow man surveys everything on the ground, with sureness and knowledge he looks all around. Steel to steel the cables he rigs. He's going to raise that monster from out of the digs. Take up some slack here, tighten it there, here comes that tractor and trailer both rising in the air. Sixty thousand pounds of might rising up into the night. He's feeling good, he knows he's right.

People follow slowly down the road. That tow truck's pulling a mighty load. Blackness of the night broken by the flashes, they follow the remains of another of the crashes. They follow along, they can't help but wonder what went wrong. They pray to God and it's understood, it wasn't them and they feel good.

REQUIEM FOR LENA

Her clothes are hanging on a makeshift rope line, summer
dresses blowing lightly in the wind. Her costume jewelry's on a
table displayed for another owner. Some will buy in memory,
others because it's almost free. Years of hobbies packed up in a
box, books to read, kitchen ware, bathroom care- knick knacks
people tracks no longer to be put to use by Lena
for her body like her hobbies is packed up in a box

But her soul will ache no more for the ecstasy of peace
since she's gone to be with Jesus in that final sweet release

Many lives were touched by Lena and each will gladly admit
that while they are happy for her, she'll be missed quite a bit

Her daughters two stand bold and blue doing things they must
do. Their family is broken with the demise of mom and dad but
they do have each other and for that they are truly glad

YARD SALE screams the signs and the newspaper ad the same.
.Along with those coming for a memory and those who are in
need, come the vultures collecting with a pure motive of greed.
They feel absolutely no shame, insensitive to what's going on or
how it came to be, just getting there early enough and wanting
everything for free

Yes, the things Lena left behind may go many a separate way
but her memory will always be something that will stay
within the hearts and minds of all those she touched
all the many people who loved her so very much

Gone home Feb.4,1979 Florence, South Carolina

IRVING ISRAEL, ESSENCE OF LOVE

A man lives his whole life to become
what he is at his final moments.
I did not know Irving Israel for most of his life but
I did know what he became

No doubt as an attorney he had his share of ups and downs.
Who hasn't? Certainly he suffered greatly physically but he did
not speak of his suffering as doom and gloom

He was a man, a kind man, a loving man. He was a father who talked often
and proudly of the children and grandchildren he loved.

He was a husband to Norma,
who brought him more happiness in eight years than most know in a
lifetime of marriage

He was a friend to many
in the fullest sense of that word
He took life's punches on the chin
and never lost his smile
He hungered to know truth in every direction and pursued it with vigor

He especially desired to know the truth of God's love
and in the end found it

His body no longer lives
his soul will live forever
his memory will live with all who loved him

I pray that we who knew him and loved him
will not allow the pain of death to cheat us out of keeping Irv's memory
alive and always a part of us

Yes, a man spends a lifetime to become what he is in his final moments
In Irving Israel's final moments at 71 years of age
he was the essence of love
and it takes a lifetime to become as loving as he was

Oct 1995 Hilton Head Island, South Carolina

MARY'S POEM

Born into Southern royalty
with tradition in every room
bound for a life laid out for her
which gave her no way to bloom

Her thoughts on yesterday's lifestyle
don't hold her firm today
for she has that special courage
to change in the wisdom of His way

She's filed away her yesterdays,
has hopes about her tomorrows
She's living full her days
Learning God's ways

Each birthday finds her wiser
in the awareness of her uniqueness,
and each new day brings her understanding
in her own personal quest

She's reaching for the universe
with the Creator she's at home
She needs no human to guide her
for she trusts in God alone

She's an ever changing woman
shedding tradition that suffocates
laced with knowledge from above
matching old and new in a life that she creates

Mary F Hilton Head Island , South Carolina, circa 1979
A friend when we really needed one!

DIVIDED

Republicans and Democrats
upper-class middle class
and no class at all

White collars, blue collars
t-shirts and sweat
the ways we divide ourselves
we will one day regret

We are equal before God
we are sister and brother
but not to each other

Will we ever be able to find common ground
where division is nowhere around?

Protestants, Catholics, Muslims, Hindus and Jews
Blacks, Whites, Yellows, Browns and Reds
all unique but we allow our colors to be negatives
in our hearts and our heads

We learn to hate one another
We long for peace but we kill off our brothers

Everyone wants but no one will give
One day soon we will regret how we live

Yes, we are equal before God but not to each other
How do we truly become like sister and brother?

PROGRESS

It used to be said
"Invent a better mouse trap
and grow rich."

for we were afraid of mice

Now it is said
"Invent a better lock
and grow rich."

For we are afraid of each other

NOURISHMENT

Drink the nectar of truth,
Sip on the wine of sincerity,
Eat the fruit of honesty,
Break the bread of candor
So that we will never
Excrete lies.

DON'T DO IT.... PRAY

There comes a time in most everyone's life
when too many problems we must face.
It is then that the world can seem
like a horrible and dangerous place.

The beauty of the world, the light of the sun,
from our life they seem to have run.
You see no beauty out of your window.
You have nowhere to go outside your door.

Life itself has no meaning any more.
You tell yourself that there are others
who are much worse off than you.
But still you don't know what to do.

The pills or the gun in your drawer
are a powerful lure, and part of you says it's the cure.
But you think of the lives dependent on you,
and you know that's not the thing to do.

You lay your body upon the bed, you close your eyes,
but you can't clear your head.
The last conscious thought that you can recall is,
"Dear God, tomorrow please let me find
an answer or the strength to deal with it all."

MEN DON'T CRY

I need the relief
the desired, required
demanded relief
which only tears
can release
building inside of me

my pulse is racing
my heart is pounding
my breathing is shallow
and swift
and all at once
I am still
As "Men don't Cry"
echoes in my mind.
Perhaps, next time!

I STAYED WITH MYSELF TODAY

I stayed with myself today
experiencing the awkwardness
of new growth and
the awareness of changes within

Through the shedding of self destructive ways
the unfamiliar process of nurturing myself
gives me a new found peace

as I allowed the tears to come.
I stayed with myself today!

PEOPLE

People walk by
with a straight forward stare.
One can only wonder
if ever they care.

A stranger's face
bearing no smile
seems all I can see
mile after mile.

People are funny
most are in a hurry.
I give them a smile
and they seem to worry.

What does it take
to make them comprehend
I mean them no harm,
I'm a potential friend?

At first we are strangers,
this is true,
but isn't a stranger
just a potential
friend that is new?

Life would be so much better
if we could all treat each other's
as if we really were
sisters and brothers.

ALMOST-MOTHER, FATHER-ALMOST

I know it was hard for you
remember, I am now a parent too.

After years of being
so far apart,
we reached out
for each other's heart.

Years of memories,
we wanted to share.
I could hardly wait to
get there.

Things were fine
at the start.
I thought we'd found our way
to each other's heart.

Then we argued about
things that were
best forgot.
I spent the rest of the time
just watching the clock.

Lifestyles so different,
so far apart, kept us from reaching
each others heart.

Although we don't love as
a parent and adult-child could

please understand
that it is
understood!

EXPRESSIONS
OF
LOVE
AND
FRIENDSHIP

LOVE IS

Love is
Joy
Peace
Excitement
Communication
Understanding
Acceptance
Heaven

Love is
Sorrow
Conflict
Frustration
Silence
Confusion
Rejection
Hell

Love is
heaven and hell
a mixture of both
blended well
fantasy, reality
strength, weakness
life, death.

Love is you!
Love is me!

LOVE IS A PEACE THAT COMES

Love is a peace that comes
from conversation in which we relate
all we have to say
and know we are being heard

from security in the knowledge
that we are being ourselves
and accepted for who we are

from understanding that we are individuals
and it is impossible
to be everything to each other

from growth
which is allowed to occur
at our own speed

from passion
which is encouraged to occur naturally
with no resentment if it doesn't

from gentleness
in a world where gentleness
too often is unimportant

from commitment
to each other as friends and lovers
today and all of our tomorrows
Love is a peace that comes!

1978 for Arlene Bridges Samuels

LOVE BEGINS

Love begins like the morning sun
easing into sight, like the first drop
of a rainstorm falling in the night.
And when it comes, it's right!
Blooming like a flower
kissed by a pure ray of sun,
blending like the rivers
which a droplet had begun…
uniting the two of us
in a love
which makes us one.

LOVE TIDE

When the sea meets the shore
they are blended as one.
At least for a while.

This is not by choice but by destiny.
So it seems with our lives,
like the sea and the shore
the tide of time uncontrolled by us
for now, makes us two again.

Try as you will to hold it back
the tide will come again and again
of this there is no choice

To drown would be an end
yet we swim.

LOVE'S MEMORY

I sit alone where we used to go hoping
against hope that you will show
but it's somewhere else you chose to go,
and the fault is mine, we both know.

Living in memory of you and me
is sometimes a nice place to be.
I let my mind wander, just set it free,
and again you are here beside me
just the way it used to be.

Our time together was happy, hardly ever sad,
except for the ending, that was really bad
for no ending of love is ever glad

Wherever you are , whatever you're doing
I pray you'll find that dream you're pursuing.
Don't worry about me, I know what I'm doing
living it over–the memories improving.

SPOONS

I found three of your spoons tonight
while I was washing dishes from the first
real meal I cooked since you left.

I thought I really wanted to be alone
until your spoons reminded me
of how we both used to call this place home

I wanted to call you and invite you over
but I was afraid of your "No"
and I didn't want to take advantage
of your possible "Yes"
So I just washed your spoons
half a dozen times or so.

HANDS

I watched them holding hands.
Hands entangled
in the rhythm of the music.

Hands and arms
 dancing on the table
with each other
And faces of love
locked in each other's eyes

Smiling and living the rhythm
of the band

Neither of them aware
of his wheel chair

GROW OLD WITH ME

We stood beneath a full moon sky
looking out at the reflections
of an ocean reaching for shore,
my love and I.

She said, "One day I'd like to paint
this beauty I see, one day when I've time."

"Perhaps," I said, "we can spend our last days
together painting our individual ways and..."

then she pulled me close and shed
her happy tears, saying

"No one ever said they wanted
to grow old with me...Thank you."

PRIVACY SWEET PRIVACY

Alone! Alone!
It's so good to be alone!
Free to think a thousand different thoughts,
Instantly understood,
and not required to verbalize a single one.

Privacy, Sweet Privacy!
Free to hear a bird sing, the ocean's flow,
the beat of my heart, and silence.

Privacy, Sweet Privacy!
Free to feel the coolness of wind blowing through my hair,
to notice the ever changing scents of the air I breathe
and to fulfill my every need

Privacy, Sweet Privacy!
Free to take a walk, lay on the beach, go to a movie,
read a book, watch TV, pray, write poetry
or just to think only of me.

Privacy, Sweet Privacy!
If I take too much, I lose you,
too little and I lose sight of me.
It's so nice to be involved with someone
who is secure enough so that both of us are free,
Free to enjoy our

Privacy, Sweet Privacy!
Alone, alone,
It's so good to be alone!

(Dedicated to Arlene Bridges Samuels)

76

TODAY'S YOUR BIRTHDAY

I heard you say, "I'm a year older today."
But, really, you shouldn't` think of this day that way.

Today is a day unlike any other day of the year.
Today is your Birth Day; the day God brought you
here.

It's a day to take notice of the years gone by.
A day to relive them in your mind's eye.

It's a new year's day belonging only to you.
It's a day to start fresh, to feel brand new.

It's the one day in three hundred and sixty five,
when you really take notice that you are alive.

It's the one special day out of the year
when people in your life can show you they care.

So have a Happy Birthday, Love,
and remember that He is taking notice above

And by His will may you have many, many more
Special days of love.

DREAMERS

She was a cashier who wanted to be a singer
I was a salesman who wanted to be a poet.
Two lonely people as yet unaware
that someone was coming for whom we would care.

I stopped at her restaurant to eat one day
and got lost in her eyes when I went to pay.
We sat and we talked open and true
both of us experiencing something new.

She was a pacifist, loyal and true
I lived in a world where one had to be cruel
She had a Masters degree from a fine school
I learned everything by the "hard knocks rule."

As our love slowly grew and peace filled our hearts
we found it easy from old fears to part.
We found ourselves able to care
This was something we'd previously not dare.

I would listen to her sing her songs
She would listen to my poetry.
Both of us expressed the same desire
to have a love that would remain afire.

She was a cashier who wanted to be a singer
I was a salesman who wanted to be a poet
I am a poet in love with a singer
we have each other and we know it.

1976 Atlanta, Georgia

SPRING IN MY HEART

Spring isn't here yet- I know that is true
It's January and it's just a nice day
Yet I can't help but feel this way
You see, it's spring for me since I first met you.

The first time I saw you I knew it to be
"I got lost in your eyes" was all I could say
The last thing I expected was to meet my love that day
Yes, I'm sure you're the one meant for me.

The feeling was right from the start
on our first date I was very at ease
You were such an easy person to want to please
You brought warmth and peace to my heart

I think of you in the middle of the day
I know I should work but it's spring in my heart
And I can't stand any longer for us to be apart
So we spent the day together in a special way

Each day I'm with you, is better than the last
I wonder how I existed without you in the past
With us , there will never be a day of nothing to do
For life with you makes everyday brand new

1976 Atlanta, Georgia

LIBERATED LOVE

We talked for awhile
The words we said bringing a smile.
I touched her face, I felt her smile
I knew we'd be together for quite awhile

I kissed her lips and she kissed mine
and the months passed without any thought of time
We've found something beautiful together
I've become hers and she's become mine
and we acknowledge we'll be together for all of time.

We are together because we want to be
and in the strong cords of our marriage vows
we'll remain a committed couple my love and me

PRETTY PONY

Pretty Pony has gone away
but don't worry
he'll be back one day
Pretty Pony was my nickname
before my curls did drop
She'd run her fingers through my hair
when I had my pretty mop.

Pretty curls around my face
in a neat and natural row
she always said, "One fine day
I'll tie them in a bow."

But I beat her to the punch
for they grew to long to handle
and now my curls sit on the hearth
by a green and yellow candle

TILL DEATH DO US PART, WE PLEDGED

Till Death Do Us Part, we pledged. Not hobbies, or careers. Not friends or family. Not finances or despair. Not wrinkles or weight not sickness or sin.

Till Death Do Us Part, we pledged. Hobbies and careers have come and gone, and both may come again. But the time invested in them pales in comparison with a walk on the beach with you, my love.

Till Death Do Us Part, we pledged. Friends and family have fired a shot or two, though they did wound, and those memories still bring pain, it will never be pain enough to separate me from you.

Till Death Do Us Part, we pledged. Finances and despair, often came hand in hand and much to our surprise they strengthened our oneness more often than not.

Till Death Do Us Part, we pledged. Wrinkles and weight often made others appear exciting , but the beauty of you keeps drawing me into your eyes and there no other's beauty can compare..

Till Death Do Us Part, we pledged. Sickness and sin, the most powerful of them all, they tried, and tried, and tried.
But our love outlasted them all. And thanks to God and
His wonderful example of forgiveness, we can truly say that "Love has covered it all."

Till Death Do Us Part, we pledged. Yes, only death can break our oneness but only in the flesh. For the oath we formed will out-live the flesh and we'll walk together with our Lord through an eternity of sunrises and sunsets in the oneness of our pledge.

EARLY MORNING DISHES

I did the dishes again today
just an ordinary task in an ordinary home
where I don't live alone.

The plates held food which nourished you
the glasses held wine at dinner time
the silver was once in your hand
I think I trembled as I placed them in the stand

Your lipstick was still on the coffee cup
I guess it's soiled but it did not seem so as I held it up
The shape of your lips in ruby red
My heart was full just knowing you were in our bed

Just little things I do to show my love
your reaction to them is a blessing from above
One would think I'd fulfilled some great need
by the way you smile and delight in my deed

You'll wake up long after I depart
but I know you'll not miss the work of my heart
Yes the dishes are done, the oven is clean
I can see the smile on the face of my beauty queen

Together since 1976, I can't believe it's been that long
yet when you walk into a room my heart still sings a song
Sure there are days that I'm not aware
of your beautiful smile and your lovely hair, but they are rare.

They are days when I'm in a rush with work and other such stuff
and I leave no signs to show my love enough
But my love, let these ordinary tasks in our ordinary home
be little signs of my love which say you don't live here alone!

August 2012 for my Arlene

LONELY NIGHT OUT

A darkened room lit by colored light
creating a fantasy world where music blares
smoke is thick enough to inhale
bodies touch each other in unfamiliar regularity
and in the midst, cold lonely people
search for warmth from the false love encounters
they have become used to

SET UP

It was long ago that he was in the singles world
of games. He never even noticed he was being set up
until he stumbled into her trap.
His mind was set on trust but once again he tasted
the bitter tears of hurt

GAMES

What do you do when you are being genuine
and suddenly discover that someone is playing games
with your emotions?
Do you laugh about it?
 I wish I could stop hurting long enough to try.

NOBLE

I hope you've gotten even with every person in your life
whoever caused you pain. I hope you've gotten even and
never have to hurt another unsuspecting person

I thought it would ease my pain if I could find something
Noble about understanding the hurt you brought to me…
But I was wrong

FRIEND

Family means people

with whom I am intimate,

with whom I share that special
closeness called caring.

with whom I can laugh and cry

with whom I can be weak or strong
with whom I can be myself
sharing the various levels of love

These people do not necessarily
have the same blood in their veins
or the same color of their skin as I do

These people are friends

 You are one of my friends

For my closest friend Ned

Years ago my wife, Arlene and I, produced a line of greetings cards which sold in college bookstores. I hope you will enjoy them. Please feel free to use any which might help you to express your feelings.

**When you
smile
I feel like
every
butterfly
that ever was
is inside me**

**When I am
with you
cuddled
in our
little
corner
of the
world
I
am
at peace!**

The
Beauty
of
life
is
that
every
day
we
have
another
chance

If we don't
risk getting
hurt
we won't
discover
the gentleness
of other people

Awareness is
knowing every
part of me,
different though
they may be
and respecting each

May marriage be
a garden of growth
for both of you.
May your union
be an
uninhibited blending
of your
bodies, minds and souls

Nothing so
joyfully affects
one's life
as the
birth of another life...
Congratulations!

I cannot change
what has passed
I can only learn
from it.
Everything
I have ever done
in my life
was
necessary
for me to be
who I
am
today.

Commitment
to love
is freedom
from
singles bars,
dinners alone,
hurried embraces...
from searching
aching
regretting.
Commitment
to love
is freedom!
I LOVE YOU!

I will not live
for you or
through you
but rather
with you
in an
atmosphere
of sharing
exploring
together all
of
love's
levels

To stroll
with you
in the softness
of moonlight

To feel your
warmth
in the coolness
of night

To hold
your hand
ever aware
of your love
is to know
HAPPINESS

One
of the
measuring
sticks for
love
is how
easily
a cross word
can hurt

First thing
this morning
I thought
of you...
I lived
through
our
memories
and
smiled
I MISS YOU!

I know
you haven't
heard from
me lately
but that
doesn't mean
I haven't
thought
about you.
In fact
I'M THINKING
ABOUT
YOU NOW!

Some
relationships
don't last
the forever
we thought
they would

Yet when
everything
is at last
understood
we can
see the good

ANNIVERSARY
A remembrance
of days gone by
and a
commitment to
those ahead.
May you
share many more.

I've
experienced
many
exciting
times
but the
greatest
thrill
of my life
is the gift
of
love
from you!

In between the
hassles and deadlines o
f everyday life you
slip into
the foreground
of my mind and
I become
aware
that my cup
truly runs over

Today I thought
of
apple pie
an ocean walk
and you
not
necessarily
in that
order

So many
good feelings
are
summed up
in just
two little words...
Thank You!

SUPPOSE
A special poem to read to your children

From a young boy's face, I snitched a nose. I stuck it down between my toes. Now, what do you suppose you would do if the nose between my toes belonged to you? Would you laugh? Or would you cry? Or would you simply try to get by without a nose upon your face, and live your life in total disgrace?

From a young girl's face, I plucked a smile. I hid it down the road a mile. Now, what do you suppose you would do if the smile I plucked belonged to you? You couldn't laugh without having a smile. So you'd have to talk about sad things for awhile but maybe you would learn to get by and you'd share a smile that was in your eye

From another boy's head I took an ear. And hid it away for about a year. Now, what do you suppose you would do if the ear I took belonged to you? Would you hold your hand up on your head and not take it down until you went to bed? You couldn't wear glasses because they'd slide off your face, and you'd look awfully silly running a race.

From another girl, I got two eyes. And I hid them away in some apple pies. Now, what do you suppose you would do if the eyes in the pies belonged to you? You couldn't look around 'cause you couldn't see so you'd never be able to find out it was me. But you might one day eat some apple pies and you might just find you've found your eyes.

Then from a boy and a girl, I grabbed one mouth each and I hid them in a sandcastle on the beach. Now, what do you suppose you would do if the mouth in the castle belonged to you? You'd have to get there before high tide, or your mouth would float high and wide and you wouldn't be able to make a sound unless on the beach your mouth you found.

But, you have a nose and you have a smile and I love it when you flash it every once in awhile. You have your eyes and your cute little ears. And you've had them all for a number of years.

And you have your mouth to complete your God given face and no matter what you look like, you are no disgrace. Yes, the face you have belongs to you and here is what you're supposed to do...

LIKE YOURSELF! LIKE YOURSELF!
BECAUSE IT'S THE WAY
GOD MADE YOU

38647590R00055

Made in the USA
Charleston, SC
14 February 2015